OBSESSIVE-COMPULSIVE DISORDER

Moving From Fear to Freedom Series

Judy Lair, LPCC

Judy A. Lair, LPCC
Counselorplace Christian Counseling, LLC
6827 N. High Street, Suite 121
Worthington, OH 43085
www.counselorplace.com

Cover art by Tabitha Stone

Book Layout © 2014 BookDesignTemplates.com

Dedicated to Laurie and Sarah
For all you've shared & taught me over the years

Everything you want is on the other side of fear.

—JACK CANFIELD

CONTENTS

DISTORTED FILTERS

"I'm so glad to meet you," I said sitting down to begin the first session. "How can I help?"

Sue shamefully lowered her head mumbling. "I think something's wrong with my brain. I can't stop worrying."

"Well, you've come to the right place," I reassured her. "Getting stuck in worries can be really tough, especially when others don't understand what's going on in your head."

Lifting her eyes to mine, I saw tears trickling down Sue's cheeks.

"I feel so crazy," she confessed. "Horrible thoughts come into my mind I don't even want. I know in my head they're unreasonable, but stabbing fear convinces me my worry is real. Everything inside is telling me to run away or do something, but people around me aren't worried at all. In fact they look at me weird when I tell them about my fears."

"Everything you're describing makes perfect sense," I validated. "Obsessive thoughts can absolutely cause you to feel like something catastrophic is happening. At that moment, your entire body is desperate to make the internal pressure go away."

Taking a deep breath, Sue sat up straight. Squaring her shoulders, she asked her most terrifying question.

"Do I need to go to a mental hospital," she asked earnestly. "I'm pretty certain no sane person thinks, feels, and acts the way I do. I'd rather be locked away than put my family in danger."

"Intrusive worries can certainly make you feel out of control. But research shows most folks with obsessive symptoms don't pose any actual danger to themselves or others. Their brain just processes things incorrectly," I answered.

"So how do I fix my brain?" Sue asked eagerly.

"Before we talk about what to do, why don't you tell me about your life and struggles so I can understand your unique circumstances?"

Sue shared her story, including the years of obsessive worries and concerning behaviors. After gathering context and information about her worries and how they manifested, we developed a treatment plan focused on:

1. Educating Sue about the physiological and learned factors relating to Obsessive-Compulsive Disorder (OCD);

2. Gathering information on her specific intrusive thoughts, images, and obsessive worries;

3. Understanding how she avoids or compulsively engages in behaviors in order to decrease her anxiety; and

4. Identifying the external and internal stressors fueling her OCD.

This approach helped us put together a strategic battle plan to address the OCD symptoms as well as the pain and hurt in her life. Sue also agreed to talk with her doctor about medication to decrease the chemical factors.

Meeting a client for the first time, I'm listening to what information they're communicating, observing how they express it, and making note of why they believe the issues are taking place. Everyone interprets life through a specific filter. But what if your filter's distorted? Walking into my office, Sue believed she was mentally unstable. The obsessions felt so terrifying real that Sue felt she had no choice but to engage in the illogical compulsions just to decrease the overwhelming pressure and anxiety.

Sue did not have valuable information about OCD and how it causes the brain to incorrectly analyze risk. Therefore, she ran all her symptoms through a faulty interpretive filter. It felt like being blackmailed by a bully in her brain who placed unreasonable responsibility on her shoulders and berated her for perceived failures. Sue's family did not have the tools to understand her symptoms and support her in a positive, healthy way. Without all the information, Sue came to an incorrect conclusion resulting in the despair I saw during our initial meeting.

Sue's story is similar in some ways to every single client I've had in my office. Read the details of her life. See how OCD symptoms impacted her health, beliefs, and relationships. You may find similarities to your story in these pages and hope for your own healing.

CHAPTER ONE

SUE'S STORY

Looking back, Sue recalled living in an OCD prison her entire life. Four year old Sue couldn't get into bed until her dad took a roller brush and swept off all the microscopic germs. "Sheets dirty, sheets dirty," she'd say anxiously. Generally the sweeping ritual took 5 minutes. But when her anxiety was high, it could take up to 30 minutes before the internal pressure eased and she got that "just right" feeling allowing her to finally lay down.

Every morning before leaving for elementary school, Sue triple checked that her stuffed animals were sitting in the "right" positions on her bed. The ritual began with Sue standing at the end of her bed. She'd count the animals once, go back through the lineup again saying their names out loud, and then re-count one last time. Doing everything in 3s was very important. When older brother Josh intentionally interrupted the ritual Sue burst into tears, unable to leave the house until the sequence was complete.

The predictability and structure of school allowed Sue to feel safe and calm. Knowing when things would happen and what was expected eased her internal anxiety. She was a fairly good student, but prone to making careless errors. The teacher noticed Sue zoned out. Even after the teacher called Sue's name, it often took significant effort to get out of her head and back to the lesson.

Another ritual involved repeating a series of numbers in her head while riding the bus home. Often the bus driver had to call Sue's name several times before she realized it was time to get off. Sue's backpack was always messy and she chronically misplaced homework. Despite her inattentiveness, Sue's teachers consistently praised her cheerfulness and willingness to help classmates.

Home was a stressful environment for Sue. Mom had her own set of rigid rules to follow.

"Line your shoes up straight."

"Don't let the neighbors know we're going on vacation."

"You can't put your outside coat on the living room couch because it's dirty from all the germs in the world."

Everyone (Dad, Josh, Sue, and her younger twin brothers Jeremy and James) tiptoed around trying to follow mom's rules. Messing up meant a mom meltdown with lots of yelling and crying. At those times Sue hid in her bedroom surrounded by her stuffed animals. Counting rituals helped ease the heavy weight on her chest.

Josh was always loud and boisterous. He went into the developmental "know it all" stage and never came out. If you told him the sky was blue, he'd argue it was actually red. Trying to communicate with Josh was exhausting and Sue preferred to stay out of his way. She enjoyed playing with her twin brothers, but they were 5 years younger and always wanted to wrestle or play trucks.

The older Josh became, the more trouble he caused. One night after everyone was in bed, 14 year old Josh took the family car on a joy ride. When stopped by the police, Josh defiantly declared he was a better driver than most adults, insisting he deserved a "special" license. Josh's arrogance became even worse after serving his sentence in the juvenile detention center.

Home was an unsafe, overwhelming chaotic battleground and Sue quickly learned not to show vulnerability or share her heart. Anytime she attempted to talk about her day at school, Josh sneered, parroting her words in a sing-song baby tone. Sue especially hated the arguments between her parents and Josh. When parental conversations about Josh's latest grandiose beliefs or destructive actions got heated, Sue would surround herself with stuffed animals. Rocking back and forth, she repeatedly counted her friends until the house was silent.

Sue felt invisible at home. Josh created lots of drama. The twins needed a great deal of attention. Mom was engrossed in her own undiagnosed OCD rituals. Dad kept mom happy so he didn't have to deal with her meltdowns. Anything and everything mom needed, dad accommodated, no matter how it affected him or anyone else. If questioned, dad rationalized it was his Christian duty to support his wife in everything. Truthfully, this strategy made Dad's life easier rather than confronting mom's unhealthy self-protective demands.

Beginning each day with a headache became Sue's norm. The minute her eyes opened, she was aware of the thumping of her heart, shallowness of her breathing, and a pulsating feeling in her head. Sue lay there going through a mental counting ritual three times, hoping her symptoms would go away. One time her heart beat so loud Sue thought she was having a heart attack. Running to her parents, Sue insisted something was terribly wrong. Dad rolled his eyes, dismissing her concerns by saying, "Why do you have to always be so dramatic?" Mom tiredly told Sue to go find an aspirin herself because she needed to get the boys fed. Feeling abandoned, Sue hopelessly cried, convinced she had an incurable disease and no one cared.

One day the morning headache got progressively worse and Sue got permission to go to the middle school nurse's office. Receiving a call, mom picked Sue up. Tucking her into bed, mom brought a bowl of soup and checked in every hour.

Dad made Josh leave her alone and even sat on the bed that evening, listening to her worries about brain cancer and tumors. Sue drank in every drop of concern and care feeling cherished by her parents.

The throbbing headache continued the next morning. Afraid it was a brain tumor, Sue begged to be taken to the doctor. Dad drove to the E.R., holding her hand for 10 hours as Sue underwent a CAT scan and complete neurological work-up. Eventually the doctors reported all the tests were negative, recommending bed rest and Tylenol. Disgusted, dad dropped Sue's hand mumbling he needed to get back to mom and the boys. Embarrassed and ashamed, Sue followed dad out to the car and they rode home in silence. She experienced persistent headaches and stomach-aches throughout middle school, but kept it all to herself. Sue went through her entire 5th grade year tortured by the belief she could fall over dead at any moment.

During high school, Sue began hyper-focusing on her looks, constantly compared herself to other gals. She'd often fixate on a particular girl, negatively comparing every individual component (face, clothes, mannerisms, etc.). Each difference caused Sue to feel worse about herself. It didn't help that Josh made belittling comments about her figure and looks. By then, her parents were tired of dealing with Josh's attitude and gave up correcting him.

Sue recognized her worries were extreme. No one else seemed worried about germs or brain tumors. In fact, people teasingly said she should buy stock in hand sanitizer. Sue often appeared to be in a trance. Being lost in her head meant missing out on important conversations, making Sue feel awkward and embarrassed. The other students whispered, pointed, and snickered. Sue internalized all the negative messages, hating herself inside and out.

Junior year of high school, a video explaining different types of mental illnesses was given as a psychology homework assignment. Sue was mesmerized when the psychologist gave an overview of OCD. Connecting to the symptoms, she excitedly ran to tell her folks. Mom immediately dismissed her observations stating, "No one in this family is crazy!" Absentmindedly agreeing with mom, dad returning to his T.V. program. Nothing was ever said about OCD at home again. Without encouragement or support, Sue felt hopeless to find any help for her anxiety symptoms. The rest of her high school experience was a depressed blur.

Going to college was a breath of fresh air. Away from the toxic home environment, Sue only had her own OCD issues to deal with and even those weren't as intense. Sometimes her roommate laughingly called Sue a "clean freak," but it was done in fun and Sue learned to own her quirks. Returning home during school vacations, Sue used dad's "duck and cover" strategy: going along with mom's crazy paranoid ideas and OCD rules.

Sue met Sam, her true love, sophomore year when he and his friends helped some freshman gals move into her Young Life house on campus. Sam was everything Sue wanted in a man. He made her feel special, like the time her dad took care of her when she was sick. But Sue's insecurities kept her anxious, worried she had too much "baggage" for anyone to relationally hang in for the long haul.

Even when life was good, Sue couldn't enjoy it. She kept waiting for the other shoe to drop. Every time the OCD got really bad and Sue needed lots of reassurance, she expected Sam to walk away. But he continued to love, support, and encourage her and a few years later they got married. Ella came along and Sue was thrilled to have a little girl to love and care for. Seeing Sam dote on Ella, Sue give thanks to God for blessing her with such a caring husband and father.

As much as Sue loved being a mom, being responsible for the care and well-being of a helpless infant was overwhelming. All the normal new mom concerns and anxieties were magnified by OCD. Sue jumped at every cry, certain something terrible was happening to her child and it was her fault. When Ella was happy and content, the OCD told Sue something bad could be happening internally. If she didn't make sure Ella was healthy right now, it would be her fault if a medical issue showed up years later. But taking the baby to the doctor over and over never brought reassurance. Instead, Sue felt guilty putting Ella through multiple exams and tests. OCD always kept her in a no-win scenario.

Preparing baby formula was excruciating. Sue made the formula before bed, putting the bottles in the refrigerator for night feedings. The can of formula was in a kitchen cabinet along with Sue's multi-vitamins and allergy meds. Shortly after Ella was born, Sue set the bottles on the counter, opened the cabinet above, and got out the can of formula. Measuring formula into the bottles, Sue then added water. Finishing the last bottle a thought popped into her head.

"What if I spilled some pills into the measuring cup when I took the formula out of the cabinet? Now I'm giving tainted bottles to my baby. My tiny infant could die because I wasn't careful!"

Panic hit like a tidal wave and Sue began sobbing, loudly berating her supposed stupidity. Sue kept declaring she must not love her child because she didn't do everything possible to keep Ella safe. Alarmed, Sam ran into the kitchen asking what happened. Sue shamefully "confessed" her "wrongdoing." After examining the cabinet, Sam knelt down in front of Sue and logically explained the unreasonableness of her concern. Over and over he reassured her, insisting she couldn't have spilled the vitamins or allergy meds without definitely knowing it.

Sue was inconsolable. She believed that having the thought meant she actually did the action or at the very least that it was possible for the action to occur. That belief was terrifying.

Nothing Sam said helped Sue because logic never decreases OCD panic. Sam moved the vitamins and allergy meds to a different cabinet, finished putting the bottles in the refrigerator, and helped Sue into bed. Exhausted, she fell into a restless sleep punctuated by nightmares.

Sue recognized her worry and anxiety skyrocketed when visiting her parents. She'd nervously remind Sam to "follow the rules." The minute Sue stepped through the door, Sam watched her tense up and zone out employing her avoidance coping mechanism.

The worst triggers revolved around Ella. Mom always had lots of "advice" to keep Ella "safe." Her fear-based comments always made Sue feel like a neglectful, ignorant parent.

"Did you use hand sanitizer before you picked her up? You can't be too careful about germs with babies."

"Make sure you triple check the doors and windows every night to make sure they're locked. I just read a terrible story about a baby getting kidnapped right out of her crib."

"You're holding her too tight! She might not be getting enough oxygen if you hug her like that!"

By the end of the visit Sue was in tears. Driving home, she was lost in her head, ruminating on her numerous parental failures. Without fail, the following day Sue would begin obsessing about her physical health. Concerns included headaches, finding "lumps" on her body, worrying she was abnormally thirsty, tired, hot, etc. The constant doctor visits, tests, and new medicines put a stressful toll on the family. Sam wanted to be supportive, but felt frustrated and helpless watching Sue be internally tormented by her worries. Every test was normal, every doctor reassuring, but Sue was never fully reassured. Her OCD always bombarded her with another "what if" worry.

Sam started to chaff at Sue's illogical rules and unreasonable demands. He couldn't understand why one living room chair was "dirty" but the other chair was "clean."

"Coats get 'dirty' by all the possible contaminants in the polluted air." Sue explained her rationale. "When we come into the house, it's OK to lay the coats on the chair by the front door because that's the designated 'dirty' chair. We just have to make sure to wash our hands after touching the 'dirty' chair. Putting our coats anywhere else means I'll have to do a deep cleaning to get that item back to a 'clean' state."

In Sam's mind, coats didn't become 'dirty' or contaminated just by walking to and from the car. What began as little quirks he could overlook were fast becoming significant restrictions in the family's daily routine. Concerned, Sam gently shared with Sue his worries something was wrong about her emotional reactions and beliefs. This conversation was terrifying. Sue's greatest fear was she would become like her "crazy" mother. What if that fear was now true?

Sue shared about the video in high school describing OCD. Sam pressed Sue to seek help for the root cause of her anxiety. Feeling like a failure for not controlling the anxiety on her own, she reluctantly agreed to see a counselor.

Sue walked into my office convinced I would send her to the "loony bin." In her mind, there wasn't any other way to handle someone with crazy, illogical, intrusive, thoughts and compulsive behaviors. She'd tried to control the thoughts and anxiety for years without significant success. Sue believed she was at the end of her rope.

Every client who sits on my couch wants to know "Why can't I fix my symptoms?" Usually, clients have been looking through a narrow, distorted filter without all the pertinent information. A comprehensive treatment plan allowed Sue to gather relevant information, understand the root causes of her chemical and emotional issues, and develop a process to move from fear to freedom.

Uncovering root problems requires gathering and evaluating information from three stressor areas: Physiological, External, and Internal. The following chapters walk you through the process Sue utilized to bring healing and hope back into her life.

CHAPTER TWO

WHAT IS OCD and HOW IS IT TREATED?

"You're so OCD" has become a common phrase applied to anything judged to be excessive. An actual Obsessive-Compulsive Disorder diagnosis, however, involves a great deal more than just odd thoughts and strange behaviors. The DSM-V clinical diagnostic criteria includes:

Presence of obsessions
- Repeating thoughts, images, or impulses that are unwanted and intrusive
- Content is disturbing and upsetting
- The person usually knows the thoughts/images/impulses don't make logical sense
- Accompanying uncomfortable feelings (fear, disgust, doubt, or a need for things to be done "just right")

- Focusing on the thoughts/images/impulses take up a significant amount of time and distract the person from daily life

Presence of compulsions
- Repetitive actions or thoughts aimed at neutralizing, preventing, and counteracting the obsessions
- The person knows the actions/thoughts only lower the distress temporarily, but engage in it because they have no other solution to deal with anxiety
- Avoidance of people, places, and situations that trigger obsessions.
- Neutralizing behaviors/thoughts/avoidance takes up more than an hour a day and interferes in important activities.

According to the Anxiety and Depression Association of America, approximately 1% of the U.S. population (2.2 million) suffer from OCD. That's about 1 in 100 adults and 1 in 200 teens/kids. It's equally common among men and women. Although 19 is the average age of onset, 25% of cases are diagnosed by age 14. One-third of diagnosed adults report they first experienced symptoms in childhood. Most OCD sufferers know their worries are unreasonable and illogical. Feeling embarrassed, most folks don't tell anyone, even their doctor, about the "crazy" thoughts, images, and actions.

A genetic research study at Johns Hopkins evaluated over 800 people in 153 families. OCD occurred six times greater in relatives of diagnosed OCD patients than the control group. The occurrence of OCD was also higher for relatives who had other types of anxiety disorders vs. the control group. It's believed genes play a significant role in the development of OCD, but there are other contributing factors including temperament and environment. About one-third of people with OCD also have a disorder that includes sudden, brief, intermittent movements or sounds (tics). Hoarding and Body Dysmorphic Disorder have similar symptoms and brain distortions as found in OCD.

Research shows it takes an average of 14-17 years to be correctly diagnosed. OCD cannot be diagnosed through laboratory or brain imaging tests, although PET scans have been used by researchers to understand how OCD impacts the brain. Mental health professionals equipped with specialized training are generally required to correctly differentiate between general anxiety and OCD.

Obsessions

OCD obsessions are repeated, persistent unwanted thoughts, urges or images which cause distress or internal pressure. Everybody has random, strange thoughts now and then. For example, most of us have driven down a road and thought, "I could steer the car off this overpass right now." Shaking our heads we think, "What a crazy thought!" and continue driving, not giving it another moment.

These thoughts are quickly discarded because most folks recognize the thoughts are not true representations of their character and intent. Someone suffering from OCD, however, cannot move forward. Their brain does not process the thought correctly. A communication breakdown occurs. In my office, I see two main errors:

Thoughts = Truth: I wouldn't have had that thought if something wasn't wrong. Where there's smoke, there's fire.

Character Assignation: Only a really bad person would have this thought; therefore, I must be a bad person.

Cognitive errors heighten stress turning on the automatic fight-or-flight mechanism. Chemicals and neurotransmitters such as adrenalin, serotonin, and dopamine are released to aid in dealing with the stressor—except there's no actual event taking place. The car did not go off the road, no one was hit, nothing bad happened. One strange, random thought and now the body is releasing unnecessary chemicals increasing internal anxiety levels.

These powerful chemicals convince the person something about the thought MUST be true. It's an internal danger signal which cannot be ignored. The chemicals turn on an alarm which completely envelopes the person until they do/think something to neutralize it. Some folks experience the alarm as anxiety, others as an internal pressure, but every OCD sufferer is assaulted in some way by the fear created by OCD.

Instead of dismissing the random thought, an OCD brain utilizes circular thinking. Picture the stock exchange ticker perpetually repeating and updating financial information. Circular thinking keeps running the same worrisome thought over and over. Each time it displays, the pressure/anxiety level increases making the person believe the worry even more.

Have you ever had a song playing in your head all day? Imagine having a horrific thought or picture stuck in your head. A video playing over and over of your children dying horrible deaths from a terrible disease that started because YOU didn't have them wash their hands that one time. I've had many clients who routinely deal with thoughts and pictures of stabbing their spouse in bed with a knife. Each time the thoughts and images jump into their mind, it feels like they've been hit with an electric shock. The content and emotional impact of these obsessions cause clients to become inner focused as they try to process what's true.

I've talked with children who get pictures of their parents dying a violent death, sexual images when picking up their pencil in school, or those who refuse to eat due to worrying food will get stuck in their throat. Logic and reason will not help someone who's overwhelmed with these intrusive, anxiety-provoking obsessions. Pointing out what they cognitive know is illogical, making the sufferer feel more isolated and frustrated. Knowing something cognitively is not the same as being able to rest in truth.

Compulsions

Shows like Monk highlight odd external compulsive rituals without explaining the overwhelming internal turmoil. As the obsessive thoughts/images remain, the pressure to resolve the worry increases. It feels like being underwater and needing to get to the surface to breathe. Each second they remain submerged, the panic grows stronger.

The OCD sufferer's main priority is to decrease the anxiety caused by the chemical response to a misunderstanding of the risk. If you're drowning, you instinctively grab onto anything or anyone. Compulsions and rituals are ways people attempt to decrease the pressure/anxiety. It doesn't matter whether the answer is logical or rational, all that matters is getting to the water's surface (neutralizing the anxiety). OCD sufferers develop learned patterns of thoughts and actions which release stress and artificially lower chemicals. Over time these compulsions can become automatic and time consuming. It's like being blackmailed by a scary bully.

Ted, a devout, faith-filled client has a random, intrusive thought suggesting he hates God. Immediately the internal bully accuses Ted of committing the unpardonable sin. Heart racing, mind blank, sweaty palms, Ted completely tunes out the world around him. Internally he believes he must be sinful and worries God will punish him and his family. Images flood his mind: being brought in front of his church in disgrace, his wife taking the kids away, Ted being homeless and alone, etc. This entire imaginary story feels like it's actually happening right that moment, bringing Ted to tears.

Even if someone shows Ted the unreasonableness of his fears, he will not be able to use their words to calm down. Instead, he's learned to repeat a rote prayer over and over, promising God he won't eat or sleep until he has done "enough penance" for his sin. It can take anywhere from a few hours to a week before the bully releases him from this internal torture. During this time Ted is completely self-absorbed, distracted from work, family, and daily functional activities.

Types of Compulsions

There are two main types of compulsions: **Action** and **Avoidance**. Clients incorrectly believe they can prevent being assaulted by obsessive thoughts/images by focusing on preventing the worries (Action compulsions). If the worries cannot be prevented, clients use unhealthy coping mechanisms such as wishing or magical thinking to deal with the anxiety (Avoidance compulsions). In both cases, the brain still believes the worrisome thought is an actual threat which needs to be neutralized.

Action rituals refer to behaviors which try to fix or eliminate the perceived fear. The person truly believes they're taking steps to protect themselves and others from a potential problem. Some folks create rituals where actions are done a specific number of times in a particular order. Others need to repeat the actions until they get an internal "just right" feeling. Examples include:

Washing/wiping down things that get "dirty" or "contaminated."

Cleaning and re-cleaning the same things a certain amount of times until it's "just right."

Picking things up that are laying on the ground so as not to be "responsible" for the potential "danger" they create.

Checking something multiple times.

Confessing "sin" to a priest/pastor or turning themselves into the police for violent or scary thoughts to prevent those actions.

Avoidance compulsions and rituals are ways people attempt to distance themselves from the worry physically, mentally, and emotionally. While avoidance may help to lower the anxiety for a short time, the person still believes the danger posed by the thought is real. Avoidance behaviors can be automatically employed when any level of stress is experienced. Examples include:

Counting (specific things like steps or tasks or just repeating a series of numbers over and over).

Leaving the scene or avoiding environments where worrisome thoughts are triggered.

Touching, tapping or moving eyes in a specific sequence.

Analyzing and researching the worry and their own actions and intent.

Clients may have some insight into the validity of their obsessions, but the anxiety/pressure of not knowing for certain can push them to extreme compulsions.

> *I would check the gas oven and door locks, sometimes 20 times before I could go to bed at night. I would worry about poisoning myself and others with insecticides or cleaning fluids I may have touched. I would drive home from work, thinking that I left the light on in my office and drive all the way back to see if it was off: "It could start a fire." Sometimes I did this more than once in a day. Many of the obsessions and compulsions were based in an extraordinary fear that my aggressive impulses, my anger, would, without me knowing it, leak out. I always thought I would start a fire by being negligent with cigarettes or kill someone by being a reckless driver. My vigilance was ongoing...and exhausting. Rapoport, p. 26*

Kevin turned himself into the police station one evening, telling the officer he couldn't stop worrying he might stab his wife in the middle of the night. There was no history of ever hurting anyone, but Kevin was so worried he might act on his thoughts he wanted to be locked up for the safety of his family. Regina watches the news every night, certain there will be a story about a hit and run matching her car's description. She retraces her drive to and from work numerous times, making sure she didn't hit a pedestrian. Sometimes it takes Regina more than three hours to make the 5 mile trip home from work.

Common OCD Themes

Most people only connect OCD to strange behaviors like cleaning, checking, or hand washing. The main diagnostic component for OCD is a need for an action or avoidance to neutralize the obsession. OCD concerns often center around themes.

Main obsession themes include:
- **Contamination** (household chemicals, body fluids, germs/disease, environmental contaminants, etc.)
- **Scrupulosity** (excessive concern with right/wrong, morality, offending God, blasphemy, etc.)
- **Perfectionism** (symmetry, fear of forgetting something important, worried about losing things, need to know or remember exactly, etc.)
- **Relationships** (negative comparisons to others, worrying whether you're in the "right" relationship or whether you are "right" for each other or "good enough" for someone, etc.)
- **Losing Control** (fear of swearing out loud or yelling insults spontaneously, fear of acting on impulses to harm oneself or others, intrusive horrific images, etc.)
- **Harm** (over-responsibility for terrible things that happen around oneself or for not being careful enough to prevent harm)

- **Unwanted Sexual Thoughts** (sexual thoughts involving children, incest, homosexuality or other forbidden or perverse sexual impulses, etc.)
- **Miscellaneous** (overly concerned about getting a physical illness/disease or body sensations leading to catastrophic health issues, superstitions, unable to decide whether to keep or discard items of no value, etc.)

Common OCD compulsions include:
- **Mental Compulsions** (preventing/restoring, wishing, controlling/stopping feelings or thoughts, reviewing/analyzing/figuring out events so as to prevent harm, rote prayers to prevent/apologize, cancelling/replacing actions or words to "undo" something "bad," counting while performing tasks and needing to end on the safe/right number, etc.)
- **Reassurance** (repeatedly asking others the same questions about whether something is fine, if they still love you, etc.)
- **Checking** (driving in circles to check and make sure no one was harmed, checking locks/appliances/door, etc. over and over, rechecking written information to make sure no mistake was made, body scanning physical symptoms, etc.)
- **Washing and Cleaning** (washing hands/bathing/grooming excessively or in a ritualized way, cleaning objects obsessively,

using hand sanitizer or gloves to prevent or remove contact with contaminants, etc.)

- **Repeating** (rereading/rewriting, repeating routines/body movements a certain number of "good/safe/right" times, etc.)
- **Miscellaneous** (rearranging items until it "feels right," confessing/telling/asking, hoarding, avoiding triggers, etc.)

Each person's obsessions and compulsions are individually tailored based on a complicated mix of environmental factors including: cultural, social, and religious background, state of mind, emotional make-up, temperament, and personal history. I always tell my clients their obsessions are rooted in the values they hold dear. Fear is more powerful when a thought, action, or non-action appears to threaten important relationships.

Medications

As with most anxiety diagnoses, the goal of Obsessive- Compulsive Disorder treatment is to bring symptoms under control, lessening their impact on daily life. Research shows treatment is most effective with a combination of psychotherapy and medication.

The decision whether to take a psychotropic medication is complex. Concerns include the health and physiological effects of taking a brain altering drug, worries medication will change personality or mood, and beliefs such as taking medication is an "easy way out" or makes you "weak."

In my professional opinion, God wants us to take advantage of available resources to live a healthy, prosperous life. While I acknowledge taking any type of medication should be considered soberly, taking medication to help your brain function more efficiently is as important as taking meds for diabetes or heart issues. OCD medication provides three important roles:

1. Allows you to release/let go of obsessive thoughts more easily;
2. Reduces sensitivity to uncertainty and lack of control; and
3. Increases ability to achieve internal feelings of completeness and acceptance of risk.

Inability to withstand internal pressure and anxiety makes it extremely difficult to do the exposure work necessary to create new neuro pathways and decrease OCD triggers. It was impossible for many of my clients to engage in the psychotherapy process until they were medicated. For some folks, medication will be required to maintain healthy brain functioning their entire life. Others are able to decrease or discontinue it once they've established new healthy responses to anxiety.

Research suggests OCD is the result of inaccurate communication between the front of the brain which receives external messages and the processing area deeper inside. Taking a psychotropic medication can boost serotonin levels helping the messages to be more accurately relayed.

> *Serotonin is used by the brain as a messenger. If your brain does not have enough serotonin, then the nerves in your brain might not be communicating right. Adding these medications to your body can help boost your serotonin and get your brain back on track. (IOCDF; https://iocdf.org/about-ocd/treatment/meds/)*

Psychiatric research shows SSRIs (selective serotonin reuptake inhibitors) are generally the most effective medication for OCD. While SSRIs are also used for depression and anxiety, patients generally need higher doses of antidepressants than doses used for depression. (Koran et al.) According to the Anxiety and Depression Association of America, the most common antidepressants used for OCD are:

- Citalopram (Celexa)
- Fluoxetine (Prozac)
- Paroxetine (Paxil)
- Sertraline (Zoloft)

- Escitalopram (Lexapro)
- Fluvoxamine (Luvox CR)
- Clomipramine (Anafranil) (tricyclic rather than SSRI)

At the doctor's discretion, medications used primarily for other conditions may be prescribed to help treat OCD (i.e. beta blockers). Your doctor might also recommend combining medications (i.e. antidepressants and antipsychotic medications). It's like putting an extra boost in the laundry to help your detergent do its job.

A large percentage of folks try several OCD medications before finding one that works well to control their symptoms. It can take 6-8 weeks before the medication is at a therapeutic level. Don't stop taking your medication without talking to your doctor, even if you're feeling better. Research studies indicate antidepressants aren't considered addictive but sometimes physical dependence, which is different from addiction, can occur. Stopping treatment abruptly or missing several doses can cause withdrawal-like symptoms.

Psychotherapy

If you have OCD, you know the frustration of engaging in a ritual and knowing you have done it, but at the same time feeling like you haven't— more agonizing uncertainty: I've been checking the stove for an hour; I can see it is off, but it doesn't feel like it is off. What this tells us is that the different presentations of OCD are the result of biology setting the stage for learning OCD responses. Grayson, p. 18

While research cannot predict or completely cure OCD, there has been growth in diagnosing OCD symptoms. Understanding how behaviors and thoughts are learned and acquired provides a more effective treatment program. Once the chemical/medication piece is adequately addressed, unhealthy learned behaviors need to be unlearned.

A significant part of psychotherapy is spent helping clients identify cognitive distortions. There are six primary distortions for OCD suffers:

1. Intolerance of uncertainty: unable to tolerate any level of risk/limbo/possibility of things going wrong
2. Excessive concern regarding importance of controlling thoughts: condemning oneself for being unable to prevent or control worrisome thoughts
3. Black/white or all/nothing thinking: inability to see in shades of gray

4. Inflated sense of responsibility: taking on responsibility for preventing possible harm
5. Mind reading: negative projection, assuming others are looking at you negatively
6. Thought-Action-Fusion (over importance of thoughts): thoughts are considered equivalent to action

These distortions reinforce the OCD cycle, causing the brain's inability to process through a trigger to acceptance. They provide the basis for obsessions and rationalizations for compulsions. Clients must make an intentional decision to actively go against these distorted beliefs in order to battle OCD and gain freedom.

The goal of identifying cognitive distortions is not to ultimately dismiss them as irrational, to change your feelings, or to make you feel certain in any way...Instead, the goal of knowing which cognitive distortions you use is to clarify which losses you will have to accept to overcome OCD. Grayson, p. 102

It is essential to work with a therapist who is trained in helping clients who struggle with OCD. The underlying mechanisms of how the brain manifests and sustains the obsessions requires specialized skills in order to create an effective treatment plan. Interview potential therapists. The International OCFoundation recommends asking the following questions:

1. *"What techniques do you use to treat OCD?"*
Trained therapists mention cognitive behavior therapy (CBT) or Exposure and Response Prevention (ERP). They may use a relational style but needs to be able to utilize these techniques.

2. *"Do you use Exposure and Response Prevention to treat OCD?"*
Choose a therapist who is well versed in helping clients through ERP.

3. *"What is your training and background in treating OCD?"*
Look for therapists who have attended a specialized internship, graduate degree, or certification in a CBT program with an emphasis in OCD treatment.

4. *"How much of your practice currently involves anxiety disorders?"*
Choose a therapist whose practice consists of at least 30% of clients with anxiety disorders.

5. *"Do you feel like your methods are effective in the treatment of OCD?"*
The answer should be an unqualified "Yes!"

6. *"What is your attitude toward medication in the treatment of OCD?"*

Mature therapists recognize research states medication plus therapy can be a very effective treatment for OCD and they should be comfortable about discussing this topic.

CHAPTER THREE

EXPOSURE RESPONSE PREVENTION (ERP) TREATMENT

The leading treatment for OCD is Exposure Response Prevention (ERP), a type of Cognitive Behavioral Therapy (CBT). A client's instinctive response to pressure/obsessive worries is to avoid triggers and neutralize them with compulsive ritualistic behaviors. CBT treatment focuses on developing new neuro pathways so the brain can accurately process and respond to triggers. ERP therapy requires the creation of a fear hierarchy. Each worry is assigned a level of anxiety number called SUDS (subjective unit of distress). I use 1-10, others use 1-100. Treatment plans include confronting clients with their fears by intentionally exposing them to the anxiety without resorting to their usual compulsions. Research shows when a person remains in the anxiety/pressure state long enough, the brain learns to correctly analyze the threat, thereby decreasing anxiety to the appropriate level. This process is called habituation.

Imagine you and I are taking a walk through the woods on a beautiful, sunny day. Rounding a corner, we see something lying on the path a couple feet ahead of us.

"Snake!"

We both inhale anxiously. (I get freaked out by snakes and I'm not ashamed to admit it!). We're both at an anxiety level 8/10. What we do at this point shows the difference between brain chemistry.

My first instinct is to stay in the situation and find out what's true. I throw a stick at the unknown shape to see if it moves. It doesn't. Despite my heightened anxiety level, I very bravely inch forward until I can get a closer look.

"It's a stick, just a stick." Whew! My anxiety level drops down to 2/10.

Relieved, I can now access the logic/reasoning part of my brain and use truth to accurately assess the situation: I'm not alone, I have my cell phone, and I'm an intelligent, competent problem-solver.

I had an emotional trigger and I experienced anxiety and worry, but my brain was able to process the information sequentially. This allowed me to gather additional information and use it to analyze the true nature of the potential risk. Once that information was obtained, the internal chemical balance changed and my frozen brain began working properly again.

If you suffer from OCD, your first instinct is to avoid. Your brain believes a high anxiety level will be physically devastating, so can't gather information because your brain went into the "fight or flight" mode. The cognitive processing feature turns off as you're flooded with chemicals designed help you react to the perceived crisis. But there is no crisis. Even though you see it's just a stick, your brain remains at an anxiety SUDS level of 8.

Now you start imagining every snake in the county is headed our way and your anxiety level shoots up to 10. Experiencing intense pressure, you cannot stand there a minute longer. Turning around, you head for the car, making a vow to never, ever go anywhere in the entire world where you might cross paths with a snake. Safe in the car, images of dying a horrible death due to a snake bite flash through your mind and your body twitches violently. You compulsively repeat a tapping sequence over and over until the anxiety finally drops. At this point you are completely exhausted emotionally, mentally, and physically.

This OCD cycle repeats itself on a regular basis because the brain does not revise its initial risk assessment. Most folks do not stay in the initial anxiety long enough for the brain to recalibrate. The purpose of exposure is to give the brain time to correctly communicate and analyze the initial data to see what is true. It requires intentionally staying in the stressful situation and allowing the anxiety/pressure to build internally without resorting to avoidance or compulsions.

In this example, you needed to stay in the woods surrounded by all the fearful thoughts and images until your brain habituated to the fear. This would have allowed the anxiety to come down naturally as your brain re-analyzed the risk.

Anticipatory anxiety is much worse than actually engaging in ERP. It generally takes 10-30 minutes to habituate to each fear. Clients tell me those minutes of hell are worth the ability to experience true empowerment and control over their brain.

I've seen how engaging in ERP promotes long term strategies for approaching anxiety. Yet persuading clients to jump off the cliff into ERP is challenging. What we fear most is being helpless and alone. Instinctively we'll do or think anything so as not to feel utterly isolated and defenseless. The brain grabs onto any thought/image/action, crazy or not, and uses it to avoid those feelings.

ERP requires making an intentional choice to step into these feelings and stay there however long it takes for the brain to habituate. There has to be an underlying belief that such a terrifying strategy will bring clarity, truth, and freedom. The client must come to the conclusion these benefits outweigh the anticipated terror of engaging in ERP.

How do you get to the place of making that choice? While most clinical settings focus solely on the cognitive behavioral approach, I believe long term healing must incorporate individual emotional and relational components which provide internal motivation for ERP. Learning how to touch a "contaminated" doorknob is helpful, but it shouldn't be divorced from underlying emotional triggers which often fuel the anxiety in the first place.

A client who solely engages in exposure exercises can quickly become exhausted and discouraged about their progress. Connecting the ERP process to a godly, holistic vision of healed freedom fosters perseverance and hope. The Bible provides numerous accounts of folks who were put in situations requiring them to make difficult choices or respond to ones forced upon them.

Taken from their homes and marched off to Babylon, Shadrach, Meshach, and Abednego were put into a training program to serve King Nebuchadnezzar. By staying true to their beliefs, these men remained strong and healthy, eventually promoted to important government positions. Jealous competitors talked King Nebuchadnezzar into demanding everyone in the kingdom bow down and worship a golden statue in his likeness.

Summoned before the king, Shadrach, Meshach, and Abednego were ordered to bow down or be thrown into a furnace. This seems like an ultimate ERP test! I'm certain their hearts were filled with fear. For those suffering with OCD, their present obsessive worry feels as imminent and real as the threat faced by these men. The courageous responses of these Israelite men provides a model for facing any level of anxiety, fear, or pressure.

> *O Nebuchadnezzar, we do not need to defend ourselves before you in this matter. If we are thrown into the blazing furnace, the God we serve is able to save us from it, and he will rescue us from your hand, O king. But even if he does not, we want you to know, O king, that we will not serve your gods or worship the image of gold you have set up. Daniel 3:16-18 NIV*

Shadrach, Meshach, and Abednego's relationship with God rested on faith and trust in his love and care for them despite difficult circumstances. They had learned the cost of self-protection was too high. A life focused on preventing, analyzing, worrying, etc. keeps you from exercising faith, hope, and love—values these men held in higher esteem than their own lives. Standing firm in values and beliefs, even in the face of overwhelming fear, brings freedom because you're no longer being blackmailed by anxiety.

I encourage clients to write a similar statement to their OCD oppressor. Here's an example.

OCD, you're always in my ear telling me all the things that can go wrong. I'm going about my day and all of a sudden you pounce on one thought and send my brain circling. One fear leads to another and another. My heart's pounding, hands are clammy and I can't catch my breath. Panicked, all I do is search desperately for some way to feel better. Even when I do something and I do feel better, I know it's not going to last long because you'll soon grab hold of me once more. I declare this cycle will stop. I'm choosing to push into the fear and anxiety rather than run from it by avoidance and compulsive actions and thoughts. I'm making the choice to stand in the fiery furnace and let all the potential terrible consequences happen. I accept it will be my fault because I didn't listen to you OCD and do what you tell me I must do. As horrible as it would be if harm comes to me or someone I love, I'm choosing to risk potential harm and believe God will be with me as I deal with the consequences. I declare my trust is in God rather than in my own ability to prevent and protect.

My clients review their declarations repeatedly as we go through the ERP process. It gives them strength and courage to stand in the anxiety long enough for their brain to habituate. We work progressively through their hierarchy of fears, teaching the brain how to re-analyze risk and process fear more accurately. An excellent step-by-step description of the ERP process is found in Dr. Jonathan Grayson's book, <u>Freedom From Obsessive-Compulsive Disorder</u>.

Another important aspect of living with OCD is healing unprocessed hurt and painful wounds. These emotions form an underground ocean fueling worry. Current events tap into the ocean. Instead of directly processing current feelings, past wounds are uncovered and an OCD episode is triggered. Lowering the emotional water table means less fuel and greater energy to handle the worry. Living a joyful, productive life requires healing in all the stressor areas in your life.

CHAPTER FOUR

SUE'S PSYCHOLOGICAL STRESSORS

There's always a nature vs. nurture component in every anxiety disorder. Understanding how both sides of that coin impact you is important when creating a treatment plan.

Sue inherited a genetic predisposition for an anxiety disorder. Her mom most likely has (undiagnosed) OCD. Other family members on both sides suffer from depression and anxiety issues. Predisposition studies show a 45-65% likelihood people will inherit OCD if it runs in the family (www.Beyond OCD.org). Sue experienced unwanted, intrusive thoughts causing anxiety and worry from a very young age. The content of her worries and types of compulsive behaviors met the DSM-5's criteria for a diagnosis of Obsessive-Compulsive Disorder. It's also true the emotional climate at home triggered her genetic predisposition and had an effect on the severity of her symptoms.

Research shows emotional stressors always exacerbate any genetic tendency toward anxiety and depression.

I recommended Sue undergo psychological testing which revealed significant signs of inattentive ADHD. Having that piece of the puzzle put a lot of things in place for Sue. The National Institute of Mental Health (NIMH) lists symptoms of inattentive ADHD as:

Easily distracted, misses details, forgetful, frequently switches activities

- Difficulty focusing/concentrating on one thing
- Often becomes bored with tasks after a few minutes
- Difficulty sustaining focused attention on organizing/completing tasks or learning new things
- Trouble completing or turning in assignments, often losing items needed to complete tasks or activities
- Doesn't appear to be listening when spoken to
- Daydreaming, become easily confused, and moving slowly
- Difficulty processing information quickly and accurately as those around them
- Struggles to follow instructions.

Recent studies are changing the way ADHD is viewed and treated. The emphasis used to focus primarily on disruptive or inattentive behaviors. Advances in neuroscience are shifting the view of

ADHD from behaviors to deficits in cognitive executive functioning. This new paradigm represents a fundamental change in understanding the how, what, why questions regarding this disorder.

The old exemplar of the person with ADHD was the cartoon character 'Dennis the Menace,' a little boy who was very restless, impulsive and hyperactive, lovable but always misbehaving and frustrating his parents and teachers. The new paradigm represents the individual with ADHD in a much different and broader way: as a child, adolescent or adult, male or female, who is burdened by a syndrome of chronic difficulties in focusing, getting started on tasks, sustaining effort, utilizing working memory and modulating emotions that chronically impair their ability to manage necessary tasks of daily life. (Brown, p. 19)

Research shows an elevation in the number of folks experiencing both ADHD and anxiety disorders. In samples of children diagnosed with ADHD, comorbidity of anxiety ranged from 9.6% to 34% (Jensen, et al., 2001) and among adults it was 27.9% to 47.1% (Kessler, 2001). Sue experienced a lot of symptoms in both categories. At times she zoned out because she was daydreaming or had trouble focusing. Other times she was lost in her head doing a counting OCD ritual or an obsessive worry loop.

"Persons with ADHD and comorbid OCD tend to be exaggeratedly impaired in their ability to shift their focus of attention flexibly and to manage their activity in ways that allow adequate reprioritizing for changing situations." (Brown, p. 152)

An accurate diagnosis of OCD and ADHD allowed Sue to begin a treatment plan which accurately addressed the root causes of her symptoms. She was relieved to know there was a biological/chemical foundation. Acceptance of this fact provided grace for her symptoms and direction for treatment. We also worked together on her Executive Functioning Skill deficits. Utilizing specific systems and reminders, she was able to make significant strides in beginning and sustaining tasks and attention, improve time management skills, and overall life organization functions.

CHAPTER FIVE

SUE'S EXTERNAL STRESSORS

External stressors include anything outside one's self. Stressors can be general, ones that most people endure, or individual to the person's particular situation. These stressors often come from the social environment we're in, the roles we play and the expectations placed on ourselves and others. A person's level of stress is proportional to how confident one is in their ability to handle situations and call on necessary resources. Sue's inadequacy in handling external stressors caused her to see herself in a negative light, increasing her condemning OCD thoughts.

Parents

The family household revolved around Sue's mom. She expected everyone to accommodate her compulsive needs and quirky requests. When someone protested, mom's anxiety could push her to become emotionally overwrought, resulting in everyone feeling guilty and frustrated. Mom's inability to push past her own anxiety left Sue feeling neglected and frustrated. She developed resentment and bitterness towards mom and God, angry and sad over the gap between the mother she desired and the one she experienced.

Based on Sue's description, dad appears to be a co-dependent enabler. He catered to mom's anxiety rather than firmly encouraging her to see issues and get treatment. Dad seemed to only pay attention to the kids when his comfort level was disturbed. As representatives of God, children look to parents to meet core relational needs. Dad's lack of validation and attention greatly impacted Sue's self-esteem.

Sue's parents appeared to be blind to her obvious OCD and ADHD symptoms. Their repeated dismissal of Sue's concerns prevented her from getting treatment at a much earlier age. Sadly, Sue's quality of life and school experiences could have been radically different had she received proper diagnosis and early care.

Brother

Josh was a very difficult external stressor for Sue. From an early age, his obstinate, arrogant attitude created a stressful environment requiring a great deal of parental attention. Josh and mom had loud arguments over her "stupid rules." His tone was intimidating, his words harsh. Mom always left the room crying. Josh would boast how he would "set mom straight." He'd even go toe-to-toe with dad sometimes. The charged environment at home aggravated Sue's OCD symptoms. She'd use any pretext to get out of the house to avoid the conflict and her obsessive triggers.

College

Living at the Young Life house had lots of benefits, yet Sue still experienced some increased internal stress. She lived with 9 other gals who didn't understand OCD or ADHD. The house rules were meant to foster individual responsibility, dependability, and caring about each other. Sue found it extremely difficult to live up to her housemates' expectations, feeling attacked when she fell short. On days when her physical energy was low, Sue could barely drag herself out of bed to go to class. Leaving shoes by the door and dishes in the communal kitchen sink elicited lectures – but no one seemed to want to hear and understand what it felt like to be in Sue's shoes.

External stressors are the catalyst which ignite and elevate anxiety symptoms. Sue worked on increasing her tolerance to external triggers. She learned how to put them into the proper interpretative framework based on biblical relational principles. You can read more about critiquing your belief systems in Chapter of From the Other Side of the Couch: A Biblical Counselor's Guide to Relational Living.

CHAPTER SIX

SUE'S INTERNAL STRESSORS

Thoughts are simply that—thoughts—unless injected with emotion. Internal Stressors are the belief filters through which thoughts are interpreted, causing them to be experienced as positive or negative. Fear-based protective thinking and behaviors range from feeling a few jitters before giving a speech to the inability to leave home due to fear.

If logic alone changed brain chemistry, every OCD sufferer would sign up for a logic class! If anxiety was primarily a chemical issue, medication would solve everyone's symptoms. Since logic is ineffective and millions experience significant symptoms even on medication, there has to be an emotional component to the anxiety fueled by incorrect beliefs. A large part of my practice involves helping clients learn how to uncover their filters and critique the beliefs, conclusions, and interpretations which the brain uses to open chemical floodgates.

Most beliefs are created while still in childhood. Kids are given rules and life instructions from parents and authority figures. Sometimes children develop beliefs and behaviors as necessary self-protective strategies in unsafe home environments. Every child creates beliefs about how to stay out of trouble or be a "good _____." As kids grow older, these limiting beliefs and strategies result in guilt, shame, anxiety, and decreased quality of life. Internal stressors develop when there's a tug-of-war between rigid rules and present circumstances.

I give my clients permission to discuss the beliefs, values, and rules they've been taught to obey without question. God wants to have an ongoing conversation about our beliefs so he can point out inaccuracies. Rather than viewing it as disrespectful, God welcomes the opportunity reveal more of his heart and wisdom. Living life and making decisions based on principles you've discussed with God empowers you to speak into fear.

Genuine beliefs are uncovered by observing feelings. While I memorized John 3:16 as a child, for most of my life I actually believed Jesus' love was given to everyone BUT me. Looking at my huge list of "failures" I felt despair and sadness, especially when we sang about God's love in church. Oh, how I wanted to FEEL that Jesus loved me too. I'd get an internal or external message suggesting I let God down and my downward spiral would begin again. My incorrect belief fueled a great deal of anxiety and guilt.

It wasn't until I was on the counseling couch as an adult I examined the basis of that belief. Hurt, pain, and relational disappointments caused me to form an incorrect belief about what God expected from me. Grieving those past events decreased my feelings of guilt, allowing clarity and truth to prevail over anxiety.

Model for Critiquing Beliefs and Processing Emotions

Sue lived all her life in some level of anxiety. She knew her triggers and did her best to avoid them, yet those very actions put Sue in a catch-22. By avoiding potential people, places, and events because she was fearful of triggering an obsessive worry loop, Sue missed out on lots of opportunities for fun and relationship. Going to events meant she'd suffer heightened OCD symptoms for a week. Self-imposed isolation negatively affected her self-image and reduced her quality of life. Depression set in as she felt trapped and hopeless to change the cycle.

At home, Sue lived an invisible life, sometimes wishing she could pull crazy stunts like Josh to get attention. But going against her character wasn't very appealing and Sue knew she'd pay for it in guilt. The constant unreasonable worries, negative outlook on life, obsessive comparisons to those around her, etc. deepened Sue's belief that something was horribly wrong with her.

By the time Sue was in high school, she didn't expect much interest or support from her mother. Dad, too, was a huge disappointment. Without receiving a sense of worth and value from her parents, Sue couldn't believe it for herself. When Sam offered love and care, Sue could only hold onto a drop at a time, continuing to experience heightened levels of relational worry. Spending so much emotional energy and time managing her symptoms kept Sue from critiquing her beliefs about herself and others. It was important to spend time in the counseling office allowing Sue to process all the feelings she'd stored up over the years.

Everyone has beliefs, rules, and standards through which they interpret the world. God uses the sanctification process to uncover our inaccurate beliefs and reveal his truth for our life. Incorrect filters restrict folks from critiquing beliefs and fully processing feelings. These steps must be taken first in order to receive truth and clarity. David models this process throughout the Psalms.

Answer me when I call to you, O my righteous God. Give me relief from my distress; be merciful to me and hear my prayer. How long, O men, will you turn my glory into shame? How long will you love delusions and seek false gods? Know that the Lord has set apart the godly for himself; the

Lord will hear when I call to him. In your anger do not sin; when you are on your beds, search your hearts and be silent. Offer right sacrifices and trust in the Lord. Many are asking, "Who can show us any good?" Let the light of your face shine upon us, O Lord. You have filled my heart with greater joy than when their grain and new wine abound. I will lie down and sleep in peace, for you alone, O Lord make me dwell in safety. Psalm 4 NIV

Do you see the way David uses a process to get from head to heart? He begins by venting to God, sharing feelings about his circumstances. David was angry, yet knew God did not consider it sin. Venting allows us to purge our heart and mind of the emotions which, if stuffed, turn into bitterness and resentment. No matter how the angry venting words tumbled out, David knew God saw they were based in hurt and pain, not sin.

Once he'd purged the anger, David's heart filled with sorrow at the plight of his people in their difficult circumstances. He brought God into his sadness and together they mourned. Bearing one another's burdens lightens the pain. Connecting heart to heart allows us to know at our core that God and others also feel deeply about our pain. True healing cannot take place absent this step. David didn't received clarity and truth about God's heart for the people until after he had offered his emotions to God as a sacrifice.

This is a biblical model we can utilize today. Process emotions, critique beliefs, and receive truth from God in order to live a relational, faith-filled life.

I explain this Roadmap to Freedom in detail in my book, "From the Other Side of the Couch: A Biblical Counselor's Guide to Relational Living."

Sue spent a lot of time in my office unpacking complicated feelings about her mother. She realized many fears about caring for her own child came from never wanting Ella to feel the same hurt and pain. Every time Sue caught herself saying or doing something similar to her mother, she worried her daughter would also feel invisible.

I continuously challenged Sue to talk about the differences between herself and her situation rather than obsessively focusing on the similarities. OCD causes the brain to replay old tapes rather than updating them with new information. Eventually, Sue recognized although she had weaknesses which did affect her family, she also had a sensitive, compassionate heart and was genuinely motivated to choose loving her family more than placating her own anxiety. This insight gave her a firm resolve to press into ERP and not allow the anxiety to make life decisions.

As with most of us, Sue cognitively believed God loved the world. Yet it was hard to really FEEL loved by God because she couldn't get past all her flaws, failures, and inadequacies.

"I'm such a mess," she'd often tell me. "How can my husband and God love me?"

Every morning Sue worried her husband would finally "come to his senses" and leave her.

Unconditional love was not something she'd experienced as a child. Her OCD demanded she always watch for the "other shoe to drop." Sue couldn't just sit in happiness. Her brain always focused on when and under what circumstances happiness would end.

Sam loved watching Sue take care of Ella, often sharing his feelings with Sue. Instinctively, she'd deflect his words of praise, responding with a negative comment about herself. Sam lovingly challenged Sue to receive his heart-felt words, giving her another motivating reason to wrestle with OCD. Head knowledge doesn't give us the energy needed to fight against fear. Sue actively took the negative thoughts captive by intentionally choosing to believe Sam's words were true and allowing the "what if" worries to surround her. Allowing herself to sit in the anxiety caused her brain to habituate to the fear.

Fighting against fear always drains energy and perpetuates OCD episodes. Allowing fear to be present initially elevated Sue's anxiety, but staying in the fear without neutralizing led to a long-term change in her brain chemistry. As Sue began to drink in Sam's words, God opened her eyes to recognize the joyful truth about how he uniquely created her to love others. The gap between head and heart knowledge began to close.

1 John 4:18 tells us love casts out fear. Sue needed to move toward God's heart of love. Part of her homework included reading the book of

Psalms. I asked Sue to claim the affirmations of God's love for herself. She was to challenge the self-condemning thoughts with those truthful promises. At first it felt like a rote exercise, but understanding how OCD creates an anxiety barrier helped Sue stay in the process. Medication now gave her a greater ability to choose truth rather than fear. Each time she made the choice to believe God loved all of her, she grew stronger in pushing back anxiety.

Unfortunately, Sue's mother was unable or unwilling to make the same choices to move toward healthy relationships. Sue knew her mother loved her, but like a person who struggles with addiction, her mother needed to come out of denial and acknowledge how her OCD behaviors affected the family. When parents do not recognize and work on their own issues, they're unable to offer much relational and emotional support to anyone else. Sue made a different choice and as a result, Ella experienced a different relationship with her mother.

CHAPTER SEVEN

SUE'S ERP PROCESS

In order to successfully utilize ERP therapy, Sue needed to identify her unhealthy internal barriers and align them with God's truth. By living a life of avoidance, she had developed inaccurate beliefs about herself, God, and others. Wrestling with those Internal Stressors brought freedom and strength, changing Sue's view of herself and who God created her to be.

As Sue went through the biblical model above, she made the connection that much of her hypochondriac symptoms began when she desperately needed to feel loved and seen. The only times she experienced feeling safe, loved, and protected happened when she was sick. That's when mom and dad gave her undivided attention. Sue drank it in as if dying of thirst in the desert. When doctors declared nothing was physically wrong and dad immediately shifted his focus, Sue felt abandoned.

Sue experienced chronic disappointment in getting legitimate relational core longings met. Unprocessed disappointment fueled Sue's OCD, which responded by hyper-focusing on physical symptoms. This unconscious strategy continued into adulthood and began to threaten her marriage. When her heart beat fast, she believed it had to be a heart attack. Bruises on her arm meant bone cancer.

Every time she had a physical worry, Sue begged her doctor to do every conceivable test to rule out all the catastrophic possibilities. The time and money invested on her health concerns was overwhelming. Sue's husband Sam was frustrated at the situation, yet wanted to love his wife well. Tension and harsh words increased at home as her OCD behaviors elevated.

We spent time in counseling grieving the failure of Sue's parents to see and address her God-given core longings and emotional needs. Grief cleanses resentment and bitterness which build up when we don't process disappointment well. God also convicted Sue of the passive-aggressive ways she used to demand reassurance from others. The grief process allowed Sue to release hurt and guilt to God so she could offer forgiveness to herself and her parents. Moving past the emotionally neglected child Sue had been, she was able to embrace a vision of the healthy, strong, caring woman, wife and mother she had become.

Decreasing the internal emotional triggers which fueled the obsessions was an essential first step. Sue gained insight, clarity, and emotional strength to stop the compulsions during ERP and tolerate sitting in the anxiety. She was now ready to effectively tackle OCD anxiety through ERP.

We began the ERP process by drafting a mission statement listing:

- Why things needed to change in her life,
- What strategies she wanted to utilize,
- Who God created her to be, and
- How she wanted to do relationships.

Using these general concepts, Sue declared war on the OCD bully. It's very important to know WHY you are putting yourself through such a difficult process. Reading her manifesto before and after exposure provided encouragement, strength, and hope. A treatment goal primarily focused on decreasing the number of times you wash your hands does not provide enough motivation to withstand waves of fear. But if the reason you want to spend less time washing your hands is to spend more time hugging your kids, you've got all the motivation in the world.

Sue gave her husband a letter stating she was choosing to trust in his decision-making regarding how to approach her physical complaints. She then wrote a list of truths about God and her husband so she'd have something tangible to remember when anxiety struck. Her list included:

> God will never leave me nor forsake me.

> Sam has seen all my crazy and is still by my side and tells me he loves me.

> God will help me see what is true by opening the eyes of my heart and renewing my mind.

> Sam doesn't just blow me off, he listens, prays, and gives me a truthful answer.

Sam still listened to Sue's "what if" health worries, but then reminded Sue of her commitment to trust in his judgment about what course of action to follow. She then allowed the obsessive worries to wash over her until the anxiety level receded and she could remember how much her husband loved her.

One of Sue's core values revolved around living a "one another" lifestyle rather than a fear-based preventative one. In order to move towards that value, she had to wrestle with her instinctual self-protective OCD urges. Every day she reminded herself her worries were not actually health-related. Instead, she was making a choice between self-protection and risking into relationship.

I got the first panicked phone call from Sue a few weeks later while the family was on vacation.

> "I've been having headaches for two days. I know I shouldn't have, but I looked on WebMD and now I'm sure it's a brain tumor. I desperately want to go to the nearest E.R. and run all the tests."

"What does your husband think," I asked.

"We talked about my symptoms and he says we should wait to see how I feel when we get home this weekend."

"How do you feel about his decision, Sue?"

"Frustrated! I want to believe he's taking this seriously, but a big part of me thinks he's just blowing me off so I don't ruin our vacation. I know that doesn't sound like him, but I'm anxious and I just want to feel better now!"

We talked about the choices which led up to this call. Sue told Sam she had a headache the first day. She acknowledged Sam listened carefully to her worries and then said he didn't believe her symptoms warranted an immediate medical evaluation. Frustrated, Sue tried to accept Sam's decision by reading her mission statement and truth list but her anxiety continued to grow. Over the next couple days the nagging worry became a heart-pounding catastrophic certainty.

"How did you try and make the worry go away? I asked.

Shamefully Sue confessed she lied to Sam, telling him she needed to take a walk to clear her head. Instead she went down to the hotel lobby and used the computer to look up her symptoms on WebMD.

"Do you feel better having checked the Internet?" I questioned.

"No!" she said in exasperation. "I know in my head it always makes me more anxious, but I just couldn't stop myself."

"So this is another opportunity to make a decision which takes you in the life direction you want to go," I said supportively.

"I just so desperately feel like I need to do something NOW," Sue wailed. "I'm convinced I have a brain tumor and if I don't get help now, I will die and my child won't have a mother!"

"That would be a terrible situation for your entire family," I sympathized. "But what impact will it have on your family right now, today, if you choose to disregard your husband's assessment?

Sue agreed choosing to go to the doctor against Sam's advice would continue the old pattern of agreeing with anxiety rather than with God. We read her mission statement again, giving her the opportunity to recommit to those values. By the end of the phone call Sue bravely decided she wanted to trust in her husband's decision today, even if it meant she would die of a brain tumor in the future.

The OCD deceived Sue into believing the primary issue that day was a life or death health decision. By languaging this OCD episode in relational terms, Sue could see the choice was actually between self-protection and trust. Choosing self-protection kept her in an isolated, anxious hell. She made an intentional decision to risk dying from a potentially undiagnosed brain tumor in order to live a life based on trust. As hard as it was to sit in the worry, Sue used her core values as the strength she needed to choose her family.

The next day, Sue said she was glad she was wrestling with the OCD, but also felt really sad she couldn't immediately appease her anxiety. Growth required sacrifice on her part of not moving toward immediate reassurance. Although the "what ifs" continued to haunt her a day later, Sue did acknowledge feeling empowered by seeing she could withstand the OCD fear. Choosing to stand on principle rather than being pushed into something she later regretted strengthened her ability to make choices consistent with her values.

Sue saw the correlation between actively choosing to believe in and receive Sam's love and a decrease in her health worries. When she did get worried, it became easier to trust in Sam's judgment because she both believed and felt his sincerity. Each step of the process brought Sue more clarity in being able to see herself and others more truthfully, giving the anxiety less credibility. These days she continues to get the "what ifs," but Sue knows to head straight for the loving arms of her Heavenly Father and husband rather than her MD!

CHAPTER EIGHT

CONCLUSION

Holding onto truth when emotions are on high alert is hugely daunting. When panic sets in, we equate feeling with truth believing,

"If I feel this much fear about something, then my worry must be true. If my worry is true, then I absolutely, must, always do whatever relieves the anxiety."

Truth cannot enter into this equation. My clients are always searching for a definitive truthful answer to whether their fear is legitimate to the circumstance. What is true is no matter how much reassurance an OCD-sufferer receives, fear and worry will still return.

Utilizing a three-fold approach to OCD offers a healthy, godly, realistic strategy to live a more peaceful, happy life.

1. Talk to a medical/mental health professional about your symptoms. Learn how to best manage your individual biological/psychological factors. Getting all the information about OCD, medications, and psychotherapy gives you a variety of options to address your particular needs.
2. Understand how your External Stressors impact your life and overload your stress reduction capabilities.
3. Ask God to show you what Internal Stressors need healed. Critique beliefs that make life feel hard and difficult. Very likely you've taken on burdens and responsibilities which belong to God.

My hope and prayer in writing this book is to let you know you are not alone. Most folks are afraid to let others know about the craziness in their head, so end up feeling trapped and isolated.

Please know you are not alone.

Many, many people deal with the same condition and there are safe people who can help. Separating the OCD bully from your own personhood gives you the courage to open up and get help. I highly recommend going to the International OCD Foundation's website for information, resources, and professionals in your area.

There is always hope. Choose to believe it for you!

REFERENCES

Anxiety and Depression Association of America (https://www.adaa.org/understanding-anxiety/obsessive-compulsive-disorder-ocd)

Beyond OCD.org

Brown, T.E. (2013). A New Understanding of ADHD in Children and Adults. New York: Routledge.

Diagnostic and Statistical Manual of Mental Disorders, Fifth Edition, (2013). American Psychiatric Association.

Grayson, J. (2003). Freedom from Obsessive-Compulsive Disorder. New York: Penguin Group.

International OCD Foundation (https://iocdf.org/wp-content/uploads/2014/10/What-You-Need-To-Know-About-OCD.pdf) John Greist Clinical Professor of Psychiatry, University of Wisconsin; International OCD Foundation Scientific Advisory Board Maggie Baudhuin, MLS Coordinator, Madison Institute of Medicine, Inc.

Jensen, P.S., Abikoff, H. & Brown, T.E. (2009). Tailoring treatments for individuals with ADHD and their families. In *ADHD comorbidities: Handbook for ADHD complications in children and adults*, edited by Brown, T.E., Washington, DC; American Psychiatric Publishing, 415-428.

Johns Hopkins Medicine, Family and Genetic Studies of OCD research
(*http://www.hopkinsmedicine.org/psychiatry/specialt y_areas/obsessive_compulsive_disorder/research*)

Kessler, R.C., Adler, L.A., Ustun, T.B., et al. (2005). Patterns and predictors of attention-deficit/hyperactivity disorder persistence into adulthood: Results from the National Cormorbidity Survey Replication. *Biological Psychiatry*, 57(11), 1442-1451.

Koran, et al. (2007). Practice Guideline for the Treatment of Patients with Obsessive-Compulsive Disorder. *American Journal of Psychiatry*, Jul;164(7 Suppl):5-53.

Rapoport, J. (1991). The Boy Who Couldn't Stop Washing: The Experience and Treatment of Obsessive-Compulsive Disorder. New York: Penguin Group.

RESOURCES

From the Other Side of the Couch: A Biblical Counselor's Guide to Relational Living by Judy Lair, LPCC

App
Live OCD Free mobile therapy app (for iPhone iPod touch and the iPad) by Dr. Kristen Mulcahy

Body Dysmorphic Disorder
The Broken Mirror: Understanding and Treating Body Dysmorphic Disorder by Katharine A Phillips, MD

Feeling Good About the Way You Look: A Program for Overcoming Body Image Problems by Sabine Wilhelm, PhD

Children and Teens
Helping Your Child With OCD by Lee Fitzgibbons, PhD and Cherry Pedrick, R.N.

It's Only a False Alarm: A Cognitive Behavioral Treatment Program Workbook by John Piacentini, Audra Langley, Tami Roblek

Talking Back to OCD: The Program That Helps Kids and Teens Say "No Way" – and Parents Say "Way to Go" by John S. March, MD

What to do When Your Child Has Obsessive-Compulsive Disorder: Strategies and Solutions by Aureen Pinto Wagner, PhD

You Do That Too? Adolescents and OCD by Jose Arturo and Rena Benson

The Imaginaries by Don and Ron Bertram

The ABC's of OCD! by Kathleen Dunn

Repetitive Rhonda by Jan Evans MA

Blink Blink Clop Clop: Why Do We Do Things We Can't Stop? An OCD Storybook by E Katia Moritz, PhD and Jennifer Jablonsky

Mr. Worry: A Story About OCD by Holly L. Niner

The Ray of Hope: A Teenager's Fight Against Obsessive Compulsive Disorder by Ray St John

A Thought is Just a Thought A Story of Living with OCD by Leslie Talley

Up & Down the Worry Hill: A Children's Book about Obsessive-Compulsive Disorder and its Treatment by Aureen Wagner, PhD

Executive Function Skill Deficits

The CEO of Self: An Executive Functioning Workbook by Jan Johnston-Tyler, MA

The Smart but Scattered Guide to Success by Peg Dawson, Ed.D and Richard Guare, Ph,D.

Family Members

Obsessive-Compulsive Disorder: A Guide for Family Friends and Pastors by Robert Collie, Th.D.

Loving Someone with OCD: Help for You and Your Family by Karen J. Landsman, PhD, Kathleen M. Rupertus, MA, MS, and Cherry Pedrick, RN

General

The Imp of the Mind: Exploring the Silent Epidemic of Obsessive Bad Thoughts by Lee Baer, PhD

Coping With OCD: Practical Strategies for Living Well With Obsessive-Compulsive Disorder by Bruce Hyman, PhD with Troy Dufrene

The OCD Workbook: Your Guide to Breaking Free from Obsessive Compulsive Disorder by Bruce M. Hyman, PhD and Cherry Pedrick, RN

Why Does Everything Have to be Perfect? by Lynn Schackman, MD and Shelagh Ryan Masline

Hoarding
Buried in Treasures: Help for Compulsive Acquiring Saving and Hoarding by David F Tolin, PhD, Randy O. Frost, PhD, and Gail S. Steketee, PhD

Digging Out: Helping Your Loved One Manage Clutter Hoarding and Compulsive Acquiring by Michael A. Tompkins, PhD, and Tamara L. Hartl, PhD

Stuff: Compulsive Hoarding and the Meaning of Things by Randy O. Frost, PhD. and Gail S. Steketee, PhD

Hypochondriasis
Overcoming Health Anxiety by Rob Wilson and David Veale

Memoirs
The Boy Who Finally Stopped Washing by Judith Rapport.

Rewind Replay Repeat: A Memoir of Obsessive-Compulsive Disorder by Jeff Bell

The Thought that Counts: A Firsthand Account of One Teenager's Experience with Obsessive-Compulsive Disorder by Jared Kant

Perfectionism

Scrupulosity

Trichotillomania

Help for Hair Pullers: Understanding and Coping with Trichotillomania by Nancy J Keuthen, PhD, Dan J. Stein, MD, and Gary A. Christenson, MD

The Hair-Pulling Problem: A Complete Guide to Trichotillomania by Fred Penzel, PhD